COOL CRAFTS
CHECKERBOARD HOW-TO LIBRARY

Cool Painted Stuff

Lisa Wagner

ABDO
Publishing Company

visit us at
www.abdopub.com

Published by ABDO Publishing Company, 4940 Viking Drive, Edina, Minnesota 55435. Copyright © 2005 by Abdo Consulting Group, Inc. International copyrights reserved in all countries. No part of this book may be reproduced in any form without written permission from the publisher. Checkerboard Library is a trademark and logo of ABDO Publishing Company.

Printed in the United States.

Design and Production: Mighty Media, Inc.
    Cover Photo: Anders Hanson
    Interior Photos: Kelly Doudna
    Series Coordinator: Pam Scheunemann
    Editor: Pam Price
    Art Direction: Pam Scheunemann

Library of Congress Cataloging-in-Publication Data

Wagner, Lisa, 1958-
    Cool painted stuff / Lisa Wagner.
      p. cm. -- (Cool crafts)
    ISBN 1-59197-742-8
    1. Painting--Juvenile literature. 2. Handicraft--Juvenile literature I. Title. II. Series.

TT385.W335 2004
745.7'23--dc22

2004053117

For Your Safety

Some of the tools shown in this book should be used only when an adult is present.

Contents

Boldfaced words throughout the text are defined in the glossary.

Introduction

Welcome to the world of cool painted stuff! In this book, you'll learn how to turn ordinary items into works of art. All it takes is some paint, a brush or sponge, and a little imagination!

The first part of this book explains the materials and shows you the basic techniques. Then it's on to the project pages, where things get really fun. Step-by-step instructions help you put the materials and techniques to use.

This book has many colorful photographs of cool painting projects. Some of the projects are described in the step-by-step instructions. There are photographs of many other projects too. These will give you ideas and help get your imagination going. There's really no mystery to copying a project you like. Once you can identify the techniques used, you can make anything you see.

When you are familiar with the basics, there's no limit to what you can do. Use your own creativity and imagination to come up with new designs and color schemes. It's thrilling to be able to take something plain and make it a treasure. And, it always feels good to give a gift you made yourself. So, let's get right into it and start painting cool stuff!

Basic Tools & Materials

In this book, the basic tools for painting are brushes and sponges. The primary materials needed are items to paint and a selection of paint. Many of the things you need for painting projects can be found in your home.

Newspaper or waxed paper protects your work surface from spills and spatters. Water will be needed to thin the paint and to clean brushes. Paper towels help you clean your brushes and clean up spills. Sheets of plain paper are useful for practicing a technique or testing a color you have mixed. Be sure to check the recycling box at home for sheets with a good side left.

Plastic container lids make excellent paint-mixing surfaces. Or, you could buy a professional **palette** at an art or craft supply store. Either will work just fine.

Some surfaces need preparation before they can be painted. Sandpaper helps take the rough edges off a wooden surface. A **tack** cloth helps remove the fine dust created by sanding. Rubbing alcohol is useful for preparing glass surfaces for painting.

Often you will need to let one layer of paint dry before adding another. A handheld hair dryer lets you speed up the drying time and keep the project moving along. When you paint on fabric, you will often need to apply heat to make the paint permanent. An iron and some baking parchment will come in handy for this.

What to Paint

You can paint on practically anything! There are probably items in your home that are just waiting for your artistic touch. You can paint frames, bookshelves, bird feeders, plain canvas bags, or anything else made of wood or a natural-fiber fabric. Be sure to ask your parents for permission before you start redecorating anything, though. You can also buy items that are ready to paint. Most of the projects in this book use inexpensive items that were purchased in a craft supply store.

Wood

In this book, we turn ordinary picture frames into works of art. Once you learn the basics, you can go on to painting bigger items, like bookcases, chairs, and tables.

Glass

You can create some beautiful stained glass effects when you paint on glass items. Try painting on mugs, vases, and candleholders.

Fabric

Painting on fabric is a great way to personalize clothing and accessories. Painted lampshades, pillows, and curtains are fun and easy projects. Try painting on T-shirts, sneakers, shoelaces, or caps. For starters, try the canvas tote project featured in this book.

Papier-Mâché

An unpainted **papier-mâché** item has a surface that resembles a brown paper bag. Most craft stores will offer a selection of unpainted papier-mâché items. In this book, we show you how to paint treasure boxes made from papier-mâché.

Clay

Clay flowerpots are inexpensive and easy to paint. Use them indoors or outdoors. We'll show you how to get started with the project in this book.

Paint

Most of the projects in this book use acrylic paint. You can use acrylic paint to create designs on wood, **papier-mâché**, cardboard, paper, or fabric.

Most acrylic paints come in a two-ounce (59-ml) plastic bottle with a built-in dispenser. Larger jars, tubes, and even paint sticks are also available. There are so many cool colors, it's more fun to buy a few small bottles than one large jar.

All acrylic paints are water-based. They will mix easily with water. If the paint is too thick to spread well, just mix in a few drops of water. Because the paints are water based, they dry quickly too. That makes it easy to layer colors without having one color blend into the others.

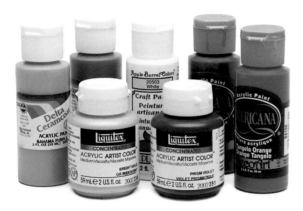

Acrylic paint comes in lots of exciting finishes too. Pearlescent acrylic paint has tiny sparkles in it that reflect light for a shimmering effect. Metallic paint has a very shiny finish, like polished gold, silver, or bronze. You can get bright, bold neon-colored paints. And for something that's even more exotic, try glow-in-the-dark paint.

Custom Colors

There's no reason to buy a huge collection of paint. Since acrylic paints blend together easily, you can mix your own unique colors. Start with red, blue, yellow, white, and black. You can mix almost any color or shade you like using these basic colors. Add white paint to any color to make it lighter.

One of the best things about painting with acrylic paint is that it is easy to clean up. It can be wiped off a surface with a wet rag or paper towel. You can easily clean your brushes with water and paper towels. However, it might leave a stain on fabric, so don't wear your good clothes when you're painting. Better yet, cover your clothes with an apron or an old shirt.

Maybe you already have a collection of acrylic paint to get you started. Don't be surprised if your collection grows. Like most painters, you will probably get inspired and want to try some new colors. Acrylic paint is available in craft and art supply stores.

The Palette

Unless you are using puffy paint, an outlining tube, or a paint pen, you will need a palette. You can buy a palette in an art supply store or a craft store. Or you can make a homemade palette by using the tops from plastic containers. They don't cost a thing and can be used over and over. Plus, you're recycling!

Here's how to use a palette. Squeeze a small amount of paint onto the palette. If you need to thin the paint, add a few drops of water and mix until it is smooth. If you want to blend colors together, put a little of each in the same spot and mix them together until the color is even.

Fabric Paint

You can use regular acrylic paint to paint on fabric. Or, you can get a special kind of paint just for fabric. Fabric paint is sometimes called textile paint. Most fabric paints require a source of heat to **set** the paint. This will make it so that you can wash the item without washing out the paint. Follow the instructions on the label for heat setting the paint.

Be Creative

The instructions for projects in this book give you suggestions for colors to use. Using these colors will let you make the item as you see it pictured. If you don't have the exact colors shown, you can mix other colors to make them. Be bold! Experiment with blending your own colors or try a different color scheme. Mix your paints into new colors and test them side by side on paper. If you like the way they look together, go for it!

Glass Paint

Glass paint is available in bottles, jars, or outlining tubes. It is specially formulated for painting on glass. You can bake the painted item in the oven to make the paint permanent. Follow the instructions on the label for **setting** the paint.

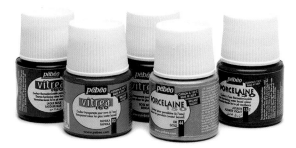

You use a brush to apply the paint from a bottle or jar. Some glass paints are **opaque** and some are **transparent**. Outlining paint is applied by squeezing it through a small opening in the end of the tube. Outlining paint is great for making raised dots.

Puffy Paint

You apply puffy paint by squeezing the paint through a small opening in the top of the bottle. You don't blend it in or flatten it out. Puffy paint creates a three-dimensional effect. It stands up a bit from the surface, which is why it's called puffy paint. It usually takes a lot longer to dry than paint that is applied with a brush.

Paintbrushes

In most of the projects in this book, a paintbrush is used to apply the paint. Any paintbrush will get the paint from the **palette** to the surface of the item you're painting. But, some brushes are better than others for specific tasks and techniques.

Flat brushes apply paint fastest, since they cover a lot of area with each stroke. They are good for making a checkerboard effect and for applying varnish.

Outlining brushes apply very little paint but let you make fine lines.

Round brushes are sort of in between flat and outlining brushes. They apply a medium amount of paint. Round brushes can be used to fill in shapes and create details. Fan brushes are used for special effects. They are especially good for creating a spattered paint look.

Use paintbrushes that are made especially for acrylic paint. Brushes can be made from synthetic materials or from animal hair. Synthetic brushes are suggested for the projects in this book. Brushes made from animal hair are usually more expensive and are not as durable as synthetic brushes.

You can do most of the projects in this book using one round brush and one flat brush. An outlining brush is nice but not necessary. The fan brush is only used for a fan effect or spattering. They're nice to have but not a must-have.

Outlining brush
(Round number 4)

Flat brush
(½ inch)

Fan brush
(Number 4)

Round brush
(Number 8)

All of these brushes come in different sizes. For example, you can get a narrow flat brush or a very wide one. For the projects in this book, we used the brushes shown above. Check out what's offered at your art supply or craft store.

You will see that paintbrush handles can be long or short. Artists who paint at an easel prefer the long handles. You'll want to choose a brush with a short handle. This will give you better control because your hand can be closer to the painting surface.

Basic Techniques

Believe it or not, all of the projects in this book can be accomplished using the basic techniques shown in this chapter.

Preparing the Surface

Most surfaces you want to paint will need a little preparation. There are two reasons for this. You want the paint to cover the surface evenly, and you want it to adhere well. Use the methods described here to make sure that your painting project will be successful.

Before you paint on wood

Maybe you'll buy brand new wooden items to paint. Or, you might find some wooden things around the house to paint. Either way, you need to prepare the surface before you paint it.

Use fine sandpaper to smooth the surface of the wood. Move the sandpaper back and forth along the surface. Sand with the **grain**, not against it. In other words, follow the direction of the natural lines in the wood.

Feel the surface from time to time, and sand until it is smooth and even. Brush off the dust created by the sanding process.

Wipe the surface with a **tack** cloth. This will remove any dust that was too fine to be brushed off. When the surface is smooth and free from dust, you're ready to start painting.

Before you paint on fabric

Wash, dry, and iron fabric before you paint it. Be sure to have adult supervision any time you use an iron.

Preparing Your Work Surface

Your work surface is another important surface that needs to be prepared before you paint. Paint is going to get on more than just your palette and your project. Use a layer of newspaper to cover your entire work area. Waxed paper can be used too. Painted edges won't stick to waxed paper as easily as to newspaper. If they do, the waxed paper rips away more cleanly than the newspaper does.

How to Use a Paintbrush

Always wet your paintbrush before you use it. Then blot it gently on a paper towel or rag to remove the **excess** water. Put a little puddle of paint on your **palette**. If you need to thin the paint, use the paintbrush to add a few drops of water. Blend in the water gently with short strokes or mix with a circular motion.

Load the paintbrush by pulling paint away from the puddle with short strokes. Keep the paint only on the bristles, not the metal part. If paint builds up on your brush, rinse and blot it before you continue painting.

Paintbrush Care

Paintbrushes will be your most expensive tool. But, paintbrushes can last a long time if you treat them with care. Take good care of your paintbrushes so you won't have to replace them often. Follow these steps carefully to keep your brushes as good as new.

- Don't let paint dry on your paintbrushes.
- Clean paintbrushes as soon as you are done using them.
- Wipe or "paint" the paint out of the brush using paper towels or paper.
- Rinse the brush in running water.

- Tap the brush gently but firmly against the side of the sink to remove paint.
- Gently blot the brush with paper towels.
- Repeat the rinsing, tapping, and blotting until all the color comes off the brush.
- Reshape the bristles by pulling them gently into their original shape.

- Store clean paintbrushes with the tips pointing up.
- You can also protect a clean paintbrush by rolling a small piece of paper around the brush tip. Fold over the top and seal the edge with a piece of tape. Store the brushes flat or standing on end.

How to Paint with a Sponge

You can also paint with household sponges or pieces of upholstery foam. Cut the sponges or foam into pieces that measure about three inches by three inches (8 cm by 8 cm). Before you paint, gather up the corners and make a little puff shape. Hold the gathered corners and use the rounded part to do the painting.

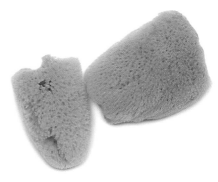

Wet the sponge with water and squeeze it gently to remove the **excess** water.

Put a little puddle of paint on your **palette**. Load the sponge by wiping up a small amount of the paint.

Tap the sponge against a piece of scrap paper to remove the excess paint. You want to see a textured **blotch**, not a solid blob of paint. If it looks more solid than textured, you have too much paint on the sponge.

Once you have the paint loaded properly, tap the sponge against the surface you want to paint. Move the sponge around and tap the surface in a random pattern.

Experiment!

Try putting different paint colors on your palette. Alternate the colors as your sponge runs out of paint.

Sponge paint with one color and let it dry. Then add a second layer of color over the first. Maybe you'll even want to add a third color.

When you use more than one color in a project, test them on paper first. Make sure you like the way the colors look together before you begin your project.

Finishing Touches

Finishing touches will help keep your projects looking beautiful for a long time.

How to apply varnish

Varnish is used on painted wood surfaces. It will help seal and protect the paint from chipping, cracking, and damage.

Use a large, flat brush to apply the varnish. Brush on the varnish in one direction only. Apply an even coat and let it dry completely. Sometimes you might want to use more than one coat of varnish. Be sure to let one coat dry before you add another.

Varnish comes in three finishes. **Matte** varnish has no shine to it. Glossy varnish is very shiny. Satin varnish is in between matte and glossy and is the most popular choice of the three.

How to heat set paint on fabric

After you heat set fabric paint, you can wash the fabric without the paint washing out.

Fabric paints are usually set using a household iron as the source of heat. Don't use a steam setting or put any water in the iron. The label on the paint container will give you the exact instructions.

To protect the surface of the item from scorching, use a sheet of baking parchment. Put the parchment on top of the painted surface before you apply the iron. Keep the iron moving around slowly. Never let it sit in one place. Be sure to have adult supervision any time you use an iron.

Flowered Minitote

This little flowered tote is as much fun to make as it is to carry. Vary the colors if you want it to match a favorite outfit.

What You Need

- Small, yellow canvas tote bag
- Flat paintbrush
- Round paintbrush
- Grass green, bright pink, yellow, and white acrylic fabric paints
- Yellow puffy fabric paint

1 Put some green paint on your **palette**. Add some white to it and mix until you have a nice shade of light green. Using a flat paintbrush, paint a wide, light green border around the edge of the tote.

2 Add pink, white, and green paints to your palette. Use a round paintbrush to add a narrow border of pink next to the light green border. Make a border of white, then a very narrow border of the darker green.

3 Use the flat brush to fill the center with light green. Use a hair dryer set on low to dry the paint before you go on.

4 With the round brush, paint small pink circles on top of the light green border and a large pink circle in the center. Paint light green dots in the white border. Use the darker green to make leaves around all the pink dots.

5 Add yellow paint to your **palette**. Make yellow dots in the center of the small flowers around the border and in the large flower in the center. Dab a dot of yellow in the center of each light green dot.

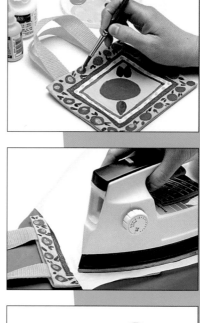

6 Heat **set** the painted surface with an iron, following the instructions on the paint label. Cover the painted fabric with baking parchment before you apply the iron. Be sure to have an adult supervise any time you use the iron.

7 Working out from the center, use bright yellow puffy paint to make a narrow line on each side of the dark green and pink borders. Rim the edge of the bag with another narrow line. Dry the bag flat for 24 hours or longer.

Practice Makes Perfect

Practice using the puffy paint on paper before you use it on fabric. It's a little tricky to make a smooth line with puffy paint. And it's next to impossible to repair a botched line. Use firm, even pressure on the paint bottle and keep your hand moving. Once you get comfortable using the puffy paint on paper, you're ready to use it on fabric.

Checkered Frame

Showcase your photos and your artwork at the same time! Painted frames make great gifts too.

What You Need

- ▸ Wooden picture frame
- ▸ Fine sandpaper
- ▸ Tack cloth
- ▸ ⅝-inch (15 mm) and ¼-inch (5 mm) flat paintbrushes
- ▸ White, purple, and bright pink acrylic paints
- ▸ Royal blue puffy paint

1 Use the sandpaper and **tack** cloth to prepare the surface as described on page 14.

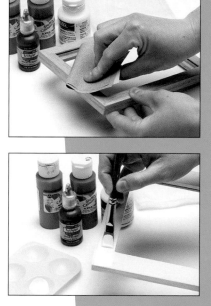

2 Use the wide, flat paintbrush to apply a base coat of white to the entire surface. The white base coat needs to be completely **opaque**. If necessary, apply a second coat after the first coat has dried.

3 Starting in one corner, use the narrow, flat paintbrush to paint the checkerboard. Use short, even strokes placed a brush width apart.

4 After the checkerboard pattern has dried, use the wide, flat brush to paint the sides of the frame purple.

4 Put some bright pink paint on your **palette**. Use the narrow, flat paintbrush to paint the inside edges of the frame pink.

5 Use royal blue puffy paint to outline the picture frame. Work out from the center so you don't smear the paint as you go. Rim the edge of the frame with a narrow line.

6 Let the paint dry for 24 hours, or longer if the puffy paint is still **tacky**. When the paint has dried, finish your picture frame with a coat of varnish.

Checkerboard Pattern

Practice using your flat brush to make a checkerboard pattern on paper before you try to do it on wood. The trick is to have just the right amount of paint on your brush. Too much paint will make it difficult to get a crisp square. Practice making your strokes the same length. Then practice making your strokes at even intervals.

Treasure Box

A treasure box you've painted is a treasure even before you put anything in it! Treasure boxes come in all shapes and sizes. You can paint the inside or line it with a matching fabric.

What You Need

- ▸ Small papier-mâché box
- ▸ Sponges
- ▸ Flat paintbrush
- ▸ Outlining paintbrush
- ▸ Round paintbrush
- ▸ White, pink, red, and yellow acrylic paints
- ▸ Plastic butterfly stencil

1 Put some white paint on your **palette**. Use the flat paintbrush to apply a base coat of white to the entire surface. The white base coat needs to be completely **opaque**. If necessary, apply a second coat of white paint.

2 Pour puddles of white, pink, red, and yellow paints on your palette. If you don't have pink paint, you can mix red and white to make pink paint.

3 Wet your sponge and squeeze out the **excess** water. Start with the pink paint and sponge it lightly on the box and the lid. Sponge red paint on the box but not on the lid.

4 Apply yellow paint to both the lid and the box. Continue sponge painting with alternate colors until you have the effect you like.

5 Use the outlining brush to paint a thin, red border along the lower edge of the lid.

6 Place the stencil on the lid of the box. Trace inside the edges with a pencil. Use a round paintbrush to carefully fill in the outline with red paint.

7 Paint the inside of the box red. Finish the box with a layer of satin varnish. Apply it with a flat paintbrush.

Working with Stencils

Stencils aren't always easy to use! Most of the time, the paint smears under the stencil. For the best results, use stencils as tracing guides. Trace inside the stencil edges with a pencil. Then use a small, round paintbrush to carefully fill in the shape. Use an outlining paintbrush for fine details.

Fancy Flowerpot

Fancy flowerpots are fun and easy to make. You can even invent your own flowers to paint on them. Fill the pot with a plant and give a gift that blooms twice.

What You Need

- Clay flowerpot
- Flat paintbrush
- Round paintbrush
- Pink, white, and green acrylic paints

28

1 Use the flat paintbrush to apply a base coat of white to the entire surface. The white base coat needs to be completely **opaque**. If necessary, apply a second coat of white paint after the first coat has dried.

2 Put some pink and white paints on your **palette**. Use the flat paintbrush to paint the rim pink.

3 Pick up just a tiny drop of white on your paintbrush. Sweep the white over the pink while the pink paint is still wet. You want to have just a hint of white showing.

4 Put some green paint on your palette. Make the leaves using smooth strokes with the round paintbrush. Don't make the leaves too opaque. Part of the natural effect comes from letting some white show through in places.

5 Use the round paintbrush and pink paint to paint the flowers. Use short, sweeping strokes that taper at the end.

6 While the pink paint is still wet, add some white paint on top. Use short, sweeping strokes that taper at the end. Don't try to blend the colors or you will lose the special effect you see here.

7 When the paint has dried, finish the pot with one or two coats of glossy varnish. Apply the varnish with a flat paintbrush. If you use two coats, let the varnish dry completely between coats.

Fun with the Round Brush

You can do some amazing things with a round paintbrush! But it's going to take some practice. Get out your scrap paper and try painting lines that get narrower at the end. To do this, pull the paintbrush up when you get to the end of a stroke. Try to paint the line and pull up the brush in one motion. It's not easy, but you'll get the hang of it with practice. These strokes are known as tapered lines. This is a perfect stroke for painting flowers and leaves.

Glossary

blotch - a spot or mark, especially one that is large and irregular.

excess - more than the usual or specified amount.

grain - the direction of fibers in a piece of wood.

matte - dull, without shine.

opaque - material that does not allow light to pass through.

palette - a thin, oval or rectangular board that artists mix paint colors on.

papier-mâché - a material made of shredded paper and paste that is molded while wet and able to be painted when dry. Papier-mâché is French for "chewed paper."

set - to become permanent.

tack — sticky. A tack cloth is a sticky cloth used in wood finishing to remove fine dust from a surface.

transparent - material that allows light to pass through.

Web Sites

To learn more about painting, visit ABDO Publishing Company on the World Wide Web at **www.abdopub.com**. Web sites about painting are featured on our Book Links page. These links are routinely monitored and updated to provide the most current information available.

Index